You're Not Alone

Registered in England No. 3056823

i

Published in: 2000

Published by: Able Publishing
                      13 Station Road
                      Knebworth
                      Herts SG3 6AP

Copyright: Isabel Hospice
                      All rights reserved

Typeset, Printed &
Bound by: Able Publishing

Additional copies
may be obtained
from: Isabel Hospice
                      Griffin House
                      Watchmead
                      Welwyn Garden City
                      Herts AL7 1LT

ISBN No. 190360706X

YOU'RE NOT ALONE

Written by:
Wendy Freeman   -   Isabel Hospice Nurse Specialist
Yvonne Johnson   -   Teacher

Co-authors:

Miranda Bowen   -   Formerly Education & Information
                        Officer Isabel Hospice
Maureen Carr   -   Formerly Family Support Team
                        Leader
Jan Meiklejohn   -   Formerly Family Support Team
                        Isabel Hospice
Caroline Tiffen   -   Family Support Team, Isabel
                        Hospice

Illustrated by Sonja Riese, Art Therapist, Isabel Hospice

IMPORTANT NOTES
FOR PARENTS AND GUARDIANS

If as a parent or guardian you have chosen to read this book, it is probably because someone close to you has died and you are looking for some help for your child.

As you too are experiencing this loss it may be important that you read the book through first, before sharing it with the child. This will allow you time to deal with the feelings it may stir up for you.

'You're Not Alone' has been written for children of 5-10 yrs old and may evoke many emotions in the reader. The book can be used to encourage children to share their feelings and fears at their own pace.

Often children don't speak about the person who has died because of their fear that it will upset others. As an adult, it is natural to want to protect children, but in doing so we sometimes exclude or isolate them. By reading and sharing the book with a trusted adult the child will learn to understand that sadness, anger, guilt and other difficult feelings are acceptable and that death *can* be talked about.

Unlike adults, children grieve in brief patches. They will probably talk about the loved person and then want to move on to talk about other things.

When children feel unable to express their feelings adults/carers may notice a change in their behaviour e.g. tantrums, sleep disturbance, bed-wetting, clinginess.

We hope that this book can help a child find some ways of managing the feelings and problems that they face.

YOU'RE NOT ALONE

This book is written for all grieving children and is
dedicated to the children who have attended the
Children & Teenage Support Groups (CATS) at
Isabel Hospice

The names and characters featured within these pages are
fictitious. However the situations represented reflect many true-
life situations faced by grieving children.

The programme for the Child And Teenage Support (CATS)
Group was inspired by Sister Margaret Pennells & Susan C
Smith's group work which began in 1988 when there was very
little structured group work for bereaved children available.
(Interventions With Bereaved Children 1995)

We would like to thank St Helena's Hospice, Colchester for their
support which enabled us to expand our Grief Support
Programme and for the imaginative idea of using stones to
portray emotions.

FOREWORD

Grief is an emotion not easily handled, even by 'mature' people, 'grown-ups!' People grieve in different ways; sometimes in ways inexplicable even to those sharing the same loss. Grief can be out-pouring and noisy, or locked-in and silent. It can be brief; dealt with, or a life sentence. We grown-ups know all this.

What then of our children? Our young ones to whom 'death being part of living' is an impossible idea to grasp (even we grown-ups avoid giving it too much thought).

A child feels loss as clearly as we do. A loved one 'gone forever' can be even more deeply mourned. We grown-ups, in the main, are better prepared for grief. We have after all lived longer – even when as young parents we are not much older than our children.

A child needs help, and patient understanding, for a child can be as locked-in as a grown-up. This little book can help, positively, It is about sharing, and caring, and finding comfort.

August 2000

David Kossoff

You're Not Alone

ISABEL HOSPICE
LOCAL CARE FOR LOCAL PEOPLE

Registered in England No. 3056823

Hello, my name is Billy and I am 10 years old.

I live in a small village in the Shetland Isles right up in the north of Scotland. There's only a Post Office in the village, so if we want anything we either have to use the ferry to go to the nearest town to buy it or we have to manage with what the Post Office has - not much I can tell you! There aren't any leisure centres or cinemas, and, even if there were, there are only six children on the whole island!

Most of the time it is a great place to be - plenty of space, the beach, the sea and boats, no noise - only the sea and the seagulls. Anyway, I like it.

A year ago my Mum died and I'm still very upset. I miss my Mum a lot, and when I think about her I'm sad. There are no hospitals on the island, and when mum had to go to hospital it was horrible. She had to go to the mainland. So when we wanted to visit her we had to use the ferry.

And then Mum died. I couldn't believe it. For days I kept thinking I could visit her in hospital - that she'd be there as usual if someone took me to see her. In the end my Dad took me to the hospital.

Mum's not there anymore. I checked everywhere. I wanted to know where she was - what had happened to her. A Nurse was there and came to talk to us. She took me to the children's ward. They have books in there, and the Nurse looked through them to find one for me. This book has been really helpful.

We sat in the quiet corner and looked at the book together. It is about a group of children who met one another because someone they loved died. I couldn't believe it, they were just like me! The Nurse said Dad and I could borrow the book for a while and that we could ring her if we have a problem.

Let me show you through the book. It's this book, the one you're reading now and it makes you very special as well. You can belong to this group too by joining in the activities. We will tell you about what we did as we go along. Rosie will start...

Hello, I'm Rosie.

I want to tell you about the group that I joined because my Nan died. It helped me when I was very unhappy.

I went to the group every week for nine weeks. I was worried at first about what we would have to do, but it turned out to be OK. We all had a drink and a biscuit while we waited for the others to arrive. The leaders were called Tim and Emma, they asked us to sit in a circle. I sat between a girl called Amelia and a boy called Lewis. We all explained why we had come to the group. I said I'd come because my Nan had died. Amelia's Mum had died and Lewis' baby brother had died. Everyone in the group had lost someone special to them. In the picture you can see the others who were in my group.
I wonder who you would sit next to in the circle?

Amelia and I got a cushion to lie on while we listened to a story about an animal who had to live without his family. He was very lonely. I felt like that too. Perhaps you feel like that sometimes, do you?

Next we did some painting. I don't like painting because I'm no good at it. It took me ages to get started. Emma said it didn't matter what it looked like. We were doing it for ourselves, not for anyone else.

I made a very sad painting. I was afraid that I had made Nanny die.

Nanny had treatment that made her hair fall out. She had funny bumps on her head and was ill a lot. After she came to stay in our house, I thought she was a nuisance because it meant I couldn't play my music or have my friends round. Sometimes I wished she would die. I felt horrible and my painting was a horrible colour when I had finished. I wanted to cry.

Emma came and sat with me and said it was OK to cry. She said it was really Nanny's illness that made her die. It wasn't my fault.

If you would like to make a feeling picture too here are some of the things you might need:

newspaper or a plastic sheet to cover the table, some large pieces of paper (brown paper, wallpaper l i n i n g paper, back of wallpaper, etc.) on which to paint or crayon, paints (poster, finger, etc.) or crayons, paint brushes (large if you can), a range of scratching tools (e.g. old match, old toothbrush), water pot.

I tried this at home.
My picture was all black.
I showed it to Dad. He said "Where are the colours?"
I said "I want my picture to be black."
When I showed it to the Nurse she said
"It's o.k. because that's how you're feeling."

9

Hello, I'm Polly.

In the first group circle I told everyone that my sister, Katy, had died. I am on my own now. I don't have any other brothers or sisters but I have a lovely pony called "Jack". My Mum often used to take me out on Jack. Have you ever had a pet which you loved like I love Jack?

Then my sister got ill, and EVERYTHING changed. Katy used to do my hair and put make-up on me. On my birthday she even took me to the cinema, but when she was ill it wasn't like that. Sometimes she was grumpy, and stayed in bed. She didn't want to play with me, and Mummy didn't want to take me out on Jack. I was left on my own all the time. Mummy kept saying, "I haven't got time. I need to be with Katy".

The only one who had time for me was Jack, so I used to go and tell him all about it. I wanted things to go back to normal, but, even after Katy died, it was still different, and Mummy still didn't want to take me out on Jack because she was too sad and tired.

The second week I went to the group meeting I took a photo of Katy and me. I wanted to remember the happy times with her, and I made a frame to put the photo in. I made my frame from cardboard and tissue paper, and I drew animals around the outside because Katy liked animals. I hope you've had happy times which you can remember.

If you would like to make a photo frame here are some ideas of things you might need: cardboard, paper, plasticene, playdough or anything else you have at home. Paints, crayons, glitter, tissue paper, scissors, glue.

Don't forget to cover the table
before you start!

I made a photo frame.
Dad helped me to find a photo of Mum.
He found it hard, going through old
photos of Mum.

Hello, my name is Lewis.

In the circle at the beginning I told everyone why I joined the group. I have a little brother. His name is George. Perhaps you have a brother or sister?

Mum went into hospital to have our new baby. I missed her. Dad left me to dress myself, but he and Gran fussed over George all the time. It wasn't fair.

Lots of people came to the house
when Mum came home
with baby Michael,
but no one
talked to me.

At bedtime Dad took us to see baby Michael, and told us that he was poorly and that he might not get better. His hair was so soft and his hands and feet were tiny.

I suddenly realised I didn't want our new baby to die. I felt all mixed up.

Lots of nurses and the doctor kept coming to the house to help Mum.

One night Dad woke us. He said baby Michael was dying. We went and sat on Mum and Dad's bed. We gave him a cuddle and said goodbye. Mum and Dad were crying. George and I cried too. Perhaps you cry sometimes too.

I feel sad telling you this and it makes me want to cry again.

Baby Michael died. Dad told us that Michael wouldn't be hungry anymore, or cry, or be poorly.

The third week in the group we were given a body picture, like the one at the end of this book so I used a black felt pen and banged on the drawing where my hands were. I felt sad in my heart so on the picture I coloured it blue and I felt glad that I'd said goodbye to Michael, so I put yellow on the head. Rosie used red for her sad colour and Polly used brown.

I learnt that "goodbyes" are special. Emma said that next week we would talk about other ways to say goodbye.

If you would like to make a body feeling picture the outline is at the end of the book. If you copy the outline onto paper you will be able to use it again if you want to.

I liked doing this one.
When I was colouring the hands I rubbed so hard
I went through the paper.
I felt really angry when I was doing it.
Dad thought I should have been more careful.
He didn't understand why I was so angry.
The Nurse spoke to Dad and explained
that a lot of people feel angry when someone
special dies.

Hello. My name is Stephen. My brother is Eric.

We came along to the group because our sister, Sarah, died. We thought we would be the only ones there who had a brother or sister who had died, but we weren't.

Lewis told us how he had said goodbye to baby Michael, but we never had the chance to say goodbye to Sarah.

She was knocked over in the street after we'd caught the bus to go to school. The ambulance took her to hospital, but she died later. She died before we finished school, so we didn't see her. No one came to get us. I wonder if you had a chance to say goodbye to your special person?

When we got home from school there was nobody there. Not even a note. We didn't know what had happened until Mum and Dad came home.

They were crying, it had all been so sudden. They told us that Sarah had died in hospital. We were very angry that we couldn't go to the hospital. We wanted to say goodbye too. Mum and Dad said they hadn't wanted to upset us and they were surprised that we wanted to see Sarah in hospital.

In the fourth week Tim told us that there are lots of ways to say goodbye. He helped us to write a letter to Sarah to say goodbye and he said that in the last week we could let off a balloon with a message too.

You can also write a letter, to your special person who died, to say all the things you wanted to but didn't. Your letter could have writing or pictures or both.

When the letter is finished, decide where you want it to go. It could be on the grave or somewhere special in your bedroom, or in your memory box.
(Have a look at the activity on page 25).

Remember if you want to change this letter one day, you can always go back and do it again, or add to it.

I had lots of things I wanted to say to Mum.
I did mine on the computer,
and I keep it in a drawer in Mum's bedroom.
I often go and read it when I am sad.

Hello, I'm Alec. My Grandad died.

In the circle I told everyone how I used to sit on Grandad's knee when he read me stories. He used to smoke his pipe, and I told everyone about his special smell. I miss this smell, but I have got Grandad's old pipe. When I go to the sweet shop where he bought his tobacco I know I can still smell him there. I like to sit in his chair sometimes because I can smell him there too.

Emma, one of the leaders, read us a story about an animal who was all alone. His family had been taken away. I liked the bit about his special memories. I have other special memories too about Grandad.

Grandad's slippers were always warm and he used to let me wear them when he was reading a story. After he died, I looked everywhere for them. Nanny said they had been given away with all his other clothes. I was very sad.

Perhaps you have a favourite place too.

In the fifth week we were able to make something to put our treasures in. Emma said we only had three more weeks in the group.

I made a box to put my pipe in. Lewis made a clay pot to put the baby's nametag in and Polly made a cotton bag for her sister's make-up.

You could make a container like I did to put your treasures in. You could use empty boxes, plasticene, fabric, paints, tissue paper, glitter, sequins or other materials for decoration, scissors, glue, needle and thread, sellotape

Your container needs to be big enough to put your precious objects in. You can decorate it if you wish. You might want to find a way to keep it closed.

I made my container out of a shoe box and painted it in orange and blue, me and my Mum's favourite colours.

Hello, I'm Amelia. I'm next to tell you my story.

I told the other children in the circle I was there because my Mummy had died.

She was ill for a long time. I helped Daddy look after her at home. The Nurse came every week. She brought me a teddy bear who was lonely and needed cuddling.

One day Mummy and the Nurse talked together for a long time, and after that she went to the hospice sometimes. Mummy got more and more poorly and then one day she died.

I couldn't believe it. I cried myself to sleep. What if Daddy died too! Who would look after me? I couldn't talk to anyone about it. My friends got fed up with me always crying at school. No one wanted to play with me anymore. Perhaps you are lucky. Perhaps you have someone who listens to you when you want to talk. Do you?

In the group I found new friends to talk to because everyone had lost someone who was special. I said I was scared that Daddy might die and then Robina told me that she worried about her Mum dying too.

In the sixth week Tim asked us if we had helped to plan the funeral. For lots of us the grown-ups did all the planning and deciding. Did that happen to you?

Robina said she had written a poem for her Dad's funeral, and she wished it had been put on the gravestone.

There was clay on the table and I used it to make a cave like a headstone for Mummy's grave. I pretended I could sit in the cave whenever I wanted to talk to her.

Polly made an angel, and because her sister hadn't got a grave, she chose a special place in her garden where she put it.

Stephen and Eric were still very upset and didn't want to join in.

Robina chose to do a painting instead.

Tim sat with Stephen and Eric and talked about how they were feeling. He said it was OK to feel angry.

Tim then gave them some bubble wrap which they used to have a tug of war and we all joined in!

This helped us get rid of our anger.

If you want to, you could make a headstone.

What will your design look like? Will you put anything on it?

You could use: cardboard, paper, plasticene, playdough or anything else you have at home.

Don't forget that you may need to cover the table.

I made a headstone.
Mum doesn't have a grave,
because she was cremated,
so Dad and I went round the garden
to choose a special place to put it.

Hello, I'm Robina.

In the circle I told the group about my Dad. One night he was suddenly taken into hospital. We went to visit him the next day and he looked awful - still and quiet. Mum and Uncle Saleem stayed with Dad, and Auntie Veda took me home.

When Mum and Uncle came home a few hours later they sat me down and told me that Dad had died. Mum just kept crying and I felt sick. All I could think about was that my problems had just begun.

You see I am good at basketball, and my Dad used to take me to the practice every week.
Maybe you have some games you like?

Dad wanted me to get in the county team. So I practised all the time - every day! Some of my friends weren't allowed to play basketball because their families were very traditional, and the girls had to stay at home.

My Dad knew I was good and he encouraged me to play. He used to tell me how proud he felt watching me but my brothers didn't like it very much. They thought I should stay at home too. I loved basketball and I still do.

When Dad died it was awful. It was as if a door had shut. My brothers wouldn't let me play basketball anymore. I felt sick. I missed Dad and I missed basketball.

After a while I wanted to ask lots of questions about how Dad had died. Uncle answered some of them, but there were some things he couldn't explain.

Tim and Emma had told us that the doctor would come in the seventh week and that she would answer our questions.

Before she arrived we played a game called ladders. We played it in two teams and the team I was in won.

When we'd finished playing we sat in a circle and the doctor talked to us.

I asked her about how Dad had died and I told her that I felt sick. I was worried that I might have Dad's illness because he felt sick too. She said that sometimes people feel sick or ill because they are so sad and when they are mixed up too. Has this ever happened to you? She said that if I go on feeling sick I should ask Mum to take me to our own doctor.

Talking to her really helped me.

When the doctor had gone, Emma reminded us that there were only two weeks left for the group.

If there are questions you would like to ask, you could talk to your school nurse, a teacher or a grown up in your family. You could ask a grown up to take you to a doctor, or ask to see a Nurse. (See the notes at the back of the book)

Dad tried to explain to me what happened, but he got very cross because I kept asking questions. So Auntie Jo suggested we talk to our Nurse again.

Hi, I'm Jade.

In the circle I told the group about my teacher, Miss Mitchell, who died. I liked her a lot. I used to talk to her about everything. She was my friend. She made me laugh.

When Miss Mitchell was ill we could only write to her. She didn't write back because she was too ill. I never saw her again and all I had left of her was the gold star she put in my book.

When my teacher died we had a special assembly where everyone talked about her.

Then everyone got back to normal. Except me.

Some days I felt as if she had never existed. I missed her so much that my head hurt and I didn't want to go to school. I wonder if I'm the only one who doesn't want to go to school when something sad happens. Am I? I tried to talk to my Mum and Dad but it wasn't the same.

In week eight Tim and Emma said we could make a favourite friend to talk to. Amelia brought her teddy in to meet us because she talked to her. The rest of us brought a sock in and made a puppet, I enjoyed this week and my puppet looks like a dinosaur. I called him Mitch and I talk to him a lot. Miss Mitchell would have liked him too.

I want to teach my friends to make puppets then we can make the puppets talk to each other and help to sort out our problems for us.

Next week is the last week of the group and I wonder what we will do. I don't want it to end.

You could make a puppet if you like.

Socks make good puppets it you want an idea to get started. What will you call your puppet?

I enjoyed making my puppet,
he looks like an alien.
I call him Spike.
That's what my Mum called me
because of my spiky hair.

Hello, we're Tim and Emma, the group leaders. We would like to tell you about some other activities we did with the children in the last week.

These were all about feelings, endings and goodbyes.

They were hard for the children to do but very important. You can see what the children said about the group on page 43.

We began in a circle. Each child was offered a bag of 3 stones to take home. The children can use the stones as a way of talking to other people about their feelings without having to use words.

It is not always easy to talk about our feelings.

One stone is about difficult feelings; one is about OK feelings; and one is about good feelings.

When the children don't want to talk, they can use a stone to let people know how they are feeling.

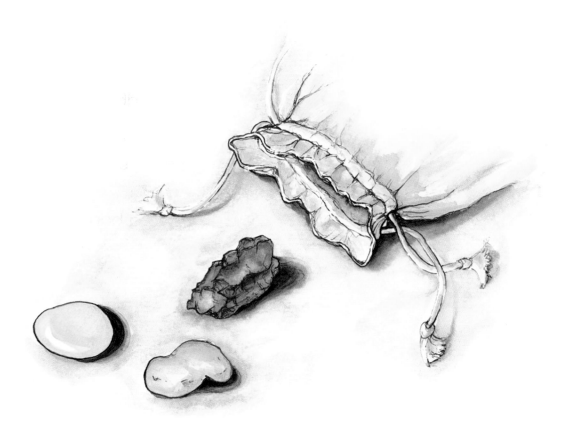

Emma will tell you about the last part of the group.

When we finish working with other people we need to say goodbye. Goodbyes can be very difficult, and that is why every week we tell the children how many weeks are left to help prepare them. However, sometimes we are not given a chance to say, "Goodbye" and things are left unsaid.

In this last week we gave the children an opportunity to say whatever they wanted to say to the person who had died. Some had things they hadn't already said; and others just wanted to say "Hello".

Each child was given a balloon and a piece of tissue paper to write a message or draw on. Then we all went to a wide-open space and let the balloons go. The children were given time and help to do this as it is not always easy.

Here are some of the things the children wrote down about the group.

I like Talking to my puppet

Jade

My photoframe I made is next to my bed and I look at it everynight.

Polly.

It was sad letting my balloon go.

alec

I liked the bubble wrap it was good. At home I have to pull and bash my pillow.

Stephen.

Same as me.

Amelia.

It was good to find other people who felt the

I paint lots at home now and they are very bright.

Rosie

Hello, this is Rosie again.

On these pages you can see a sort of party going on. We all meet up once a year. It is good to see the others from the group and find out how they are doing. I enjoy being able to talk about my Nanny to others who understand how I feel. This is the fourth get-together but this year Robina decided not to come anymore. She still thinks about her Dad but she doesn't need the group meeting anymore. I'm not sure how I feel. I wanted to come this year, but maybe next year I won't be here. I'll wait and see how I feel then.

I hope you enjoyed reading this book with me. It made me feel less lonely because I found some other children whose special person had died. I hope it helped you too.

I tried some of the activities. I liked writing the letter to my Mum and I keep it in my bedroom in a special box that I made. I read it when I am sad and I have put a bottle of her favourite perfume in so that I can smell it often and I've got a birthday card Mum gave me too.

I asked Auntie Jo to buy a balloon so that I could send a message to Mum. I wanted to tell her something but she died before I could visit her again.

We went to the beach on a windy day and I let go of my balloon with its message tied on.

We watched it for ages until it went out of sight.

BODY PICTURE

BOOKS ADULTS MIGHT LIKE TO READ:

Title	Author (Publisher, Year)
The Courage to Grieve	Judy Tatelbaum (Heinemann, 1981)
Waterbugs & Dragonflies : Explaining Death to Children	Doris Stickney (Mowbray, 1984)
Helping Children Cope With Grief	Rosemary Wells (Sheldon Press, 1988)
Talking About Death	Earl Grollman (Beacon Press, 1990)
Grief & Bereavement: Understanding Children	Ann Couldrick (Sobell Publications, 1991)
Grief in Children: A Handbook for Adults	Atle Dyregrov (Jessica Kingsley, 1991)

BOOKS CHILDREN MIGHT LIKE TO READ:

Title		Author (Publisher, Year)
The Tenth Good Thing About Barney A young boy grieves for his cat	*(3 yrs +)*	Judith Viorst (Collins, 1973)
Your Friend Rebecca	*(12 yrs +)*	Linda Hoy (Bodley Head, 1983)
How It Feels When A Parent Dies	*(7 yrs +)*	Jill Krementz (Gollancz, 1983)
Badger's Parting Gifts	*(3 yrs +)*	Susan Varley (Picture Lions 1985)
Mama's Going To Buy You A Mocking Bird A story of a death of a father	*(12 yrs +)*	Jean Little (Puffin, 1986)
A Taste of Blackberries A story of a death of a friend	*(8 yrs +)*	Doris Buchanan Smith (Puffin, 1987)
When Uncle Bob Died	*(4 yrs +)*	Althea (Dinosaur, 1988)
Grandpa	*(3 yrs +)*	John Burningham (Fox, 1990)
Saying Goodbye to Daddy	*(4 yrs +)*	Judith Vigna (Albert Whitman & Co, 1991)
Death – What's Happening	*(6-14 yrs)*	Karen Bryant-Mole (Wayland, 1992)
I Feel Angry	*(3 yrs +)*	Brian Moses (Wayland, 1993)
Remembering Mum	*(3 yrs +)*	Ginny Perkins & Leon Morris (A & C Black)

Useful Contacts

Samaritans (Head Office)	01753-216500 or 0800 555111
Gingerbread	0800-018-4318
Compassionate Friends	0117-966-5202
Cruse	0208-9404818
British Association of Counselling	01788-550899
Childline HQ (National No.)	0207-2391000 0800-1111
Child Death Help Line	0800 282 986
National Association of One Parent Families	0800 0185026
Winston's Wish	01452 394377
G.P.*	_ _ _ _ _ _ _ _ _ _
Health Visitor*	_ _ _ _ _ _ _ _ _ _
Local Hospice*	_ _ _ _ _ _ _ _ _ _
Citizen's Advice Bureau*	_ _ _ _ _ _ _ _ _ _
Social Services*	_ _ _ _ _ _ _ _ _ _

* See local telephone directory